D1187609

Houses
and
Homes

John Williams

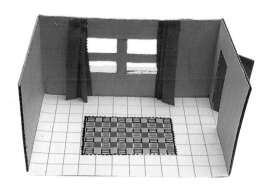

RSVP
RAINTREE
STECK-VAUGHN
P U B L I S H E R S
The Steck-Vaughn Company

Austin, Texas

Published by Raintree Steck-Vaughn Publishers, an imprint of Steck-Vaughn Company

Library of Congress Cataloging-in-Publication Data
Williams, John.
Houses and homes / John Williams.
        p.   cm.—(Design and make)
    Includes bibliographical references and index.
    Summary: Describes various parts of a home and their functions and several different kinds of dwellings with instructions for making a teepee, a mud house, a garden, a floor plan, model furniture, and more.
    ISBN 0-8172-4886-2
    1. House construction—Juvenile literature.
    2. Architecture, domestic—Juvenile literature.
    3. Handicraft—Juvenile literature.
    [1. Dwellings—Design and construction.
    2. Architecture, Domestic. 3. Models and modelmaking.
    4. Handicraft..]
    I. Title. II. Series: Williams, John, 1939- Design and make.
    TH4811.5.W55   1997
    643'.1—dc21   96-48749

Printed in Italy. Bound in the United States.
1 2 3 4 5 6 7 8 9 0 01 00 99 98 97

Commissioned photography by Zul Mukhida

CONTENTS

INTRODUCTION

People around the world live in homes of one kind or another. There are many different shapes and types of homes, from small huts to huge apartment buildings. Homes may be built of all sorts of materials from straw and mud to glass and steel.

Houses are made to protect us from the weather. Roofs keep off the rain and shade us from hot sun. Walls shelter us from the wind and cold and also keep water from getting in when it rains.

Windows let daylight come in. They can be opened when it is warm and closed when it gets cold. Doors allow us to go in and out.

Houses also give us somewhere to put our possessions. We can lock the doors and windows to keep out burglars.

These Greek houses are made from stone and cement. In the summer in Greece it can get very hot. To keep the insides cool, the houses have thick walls and small windows. The outsides are all painted white, to reflect the heat of the sun.

In Indonesia there are plenty of trees, so many houses are made from wood. In this area the rain can be very heavy. The roofs are thick to keep out the rain and sloped so that the water runs off easily.

Think about the apartment or house where you live.

- What are the walls made from? They may be wood, brick, or stone—or something else.
- How many rooms does it have? Make a list of all the rooms.
- What sort of roof does it have? Flat or sloping? What is it made from?
- How many outside doors does it have? When you go from room to room how many doors are there on the inside?
- How many windows does it have? Is there a window in each room?
- Does it have special heating? People in cold countries need heating; people in hot countries might need a way to cool their homes.

Make a list or write a story about how your home is made.

This house in Pennsylvania was designed by famed architect Frank Lloyd Wright. It was named "Falling-water" because it was built on top of a waterfall.

NATIVE AMERICAN TEEPEE

YOU WILL NEED

- Six bamboo poles, approx. 6 ft (1.8 m) long
- 10 ft (3 m) string or cord
- Old sheet or bedspread
- Large paper fasteners
- Paints (optional)
- Paintbrush

Native Americans have lived in North America for thousands of years. Some of them were hunters. They followed herds of buffalo that they killed for their food. Because they were always moving, they needed homes they could take with them. These were teepees, which were made from animal skins and sewn around long wooden poles. This teepee is made from material, because there are not enough buffalo to hunt anymore.

A teepee is a type of tent, where a covering is held up by a rigid frame. Here is a way to make your own teepee, big enough to go inside. It is probably easiest to make the teepee outside, on grass if possible. You can push the poles into the ground in order to keep them firmly in place.

1 Take the bamboo poles and hold them together. Wind the string around them, about 8 in. (20 cm) from one end. Tie the string in a knot.

2 Hold the poles upright, with the tied ends at the top. To make the shape of a teepee, start to move the ends out at the bottom.

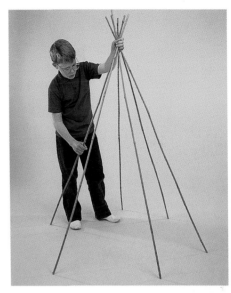

3 Gradually spread the poles to form an even circle at the bottom. Make sure they are firmly anchored on the ground, so that they do not fall over.

4 Take the material and wrap it around the frame. Remember to leave an opening for a door. It may help to use paper fasteners to attach the material to the poles.

5 Native Americans often painted their homes with designs. Decorate your teepee with the paint and allow it to dry.

NOW TRY THIS

The animal skins used by the Native Americans were thick enough to keep out the wind and rain. You can make your teepee waterproof by adding a big sheet of plastic over the material.

7

"MUD" HOUSE

Some people are not able to buy wood or bricks to build their houses. They must use whatever material they can find around them. All over the world, people use earth or clay to build walls and straw or branches for a roof. Here is a model house you can build in the same way.

YOU WILL NEED

- Wooden board, painted or covered with plastic to make it waterproof
- Potter's clay or modeling clay
- Popsicle sticks
- Straight sticks
- Straw or hay
- Tape

1 Decide on the shape of your house, and draw the shape with a pencil on the board. Start to build the walls around the pencil line.

2 Keep building up the walls. They should not be too thin or they will fall over. Leave gaps for windows and a door.

A home does not have to be in shapes like squares or boxes. Many African people build houses in the shape of circles. These houses in Nigeria are made from earth, and the roofs are covered with straw.

3 To keep the wall above the windows and doors from falling down into the gap, make a brace, called a lintel. Put a popsicle stick over the top of each gap.

4 Keep building up the walls. The wooden lintels will keep the clay from falling into the spaces left for the door and windows.

5 The roof can be flat or sloping. Use long sticks to make a frame across the house to hold up the roof. These are called rafters.

6 Use the straw or hay to make a roof. It may help to tie it in bundles first, using tape. Make some bundles and lay them across the rafters.

DESIGN A HOME

YOU WILL NEED

- Large sheets of squared graph paper
- Pencil
- Ruler
- Eraser
- Felt-tipped pens

Imagine that you are going to design a new apartment or house. It is going to have two bedrooms, a kitchen, a living room, and a bathroom.

When you are doing this, think about your own home and how its rooms are arranged.

1 Make a list of the things to put in your house. You will have to include doors and windows. Don't forget that every home needs a front door as well.

2 Draw your design on the graph paper. First, mark out the rooms. Will there be a hallway, with all the rooms coming off it? Or will most rooms open off the living room?

People who design buildings are called architects. They talk to the people who are paying for the building to find out what they want. Then the architects draw plans to show what the place will look like. While it is being built, the architect checks that the builder is doing everything correctly.

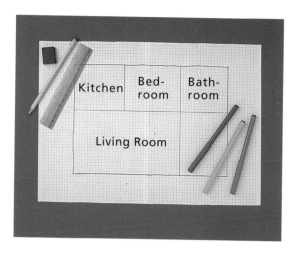

3 On the plan, write down the name of each room, for example, Bedroom, Kitchen, and so on.

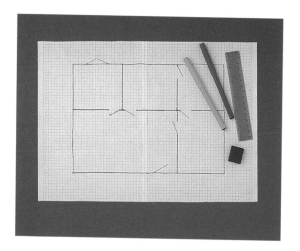

4 Decide where the doors will go. Each room needs a door, and some rooms may have more than one.

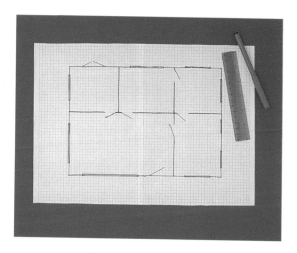

5 Then mark where the windows will go on the outside wall of the house. Each room should have at least one window.

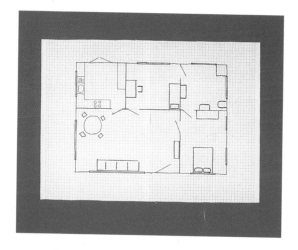

6 If you wish, you can even mark where the furniture will go. Draw the shapes of things such as tables, chairs, beds, and cupboards.

NOW TRY THIS

Using graph paper, draw a real plan, like a map, of a room in your home. It could be your bedroom, or perhaps the living room. Draw it so that 3 ft. (1 m) in the room equals one square on your paper. To do this you will need a long ruler or a tape measure to measure everything in the room.

MODEL ROOM

When a home has been designed and planned (see pages 10–11), it can then be built. Here are ideas for making a model room, with windows and doors.

A model like this is easy to glue if the glue is put on and then allowed to dry a little before pushing the pieces together.

YOU WILL NEED

- Stiff cardboard for base
- Thick, soft cardboard for walls
- Thin, see-through plastic for windows
- Glue
- Scraps of fabric
- Pencil
- Ruler
- Scissors
- Masking tape
- Paint and paintbrush

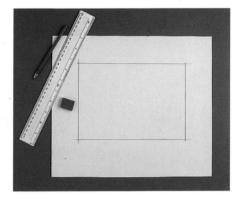

1 Find a piece of stiff cardboard. Using a pencil and ruler, mark the size and shape of the room you are going to make.

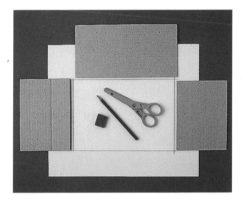

2 Measure the length of each wall on your plan and cut them out of thick cardboard. Each wall should be about 5 in. (12 cm) high.

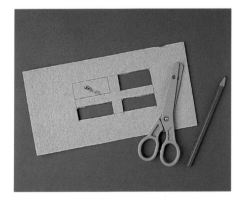

3 Draw the shapes of the windows on the walls. Cut them out. Cut a piece of thin plastic to cover the window.

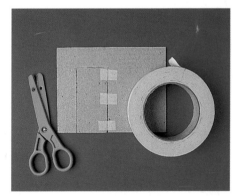

4 Cut a door shape in a wall. Make hinges out of masking tape and join the door to the wall down one side.

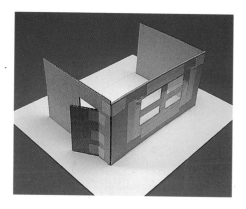 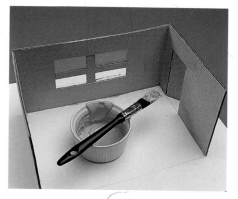 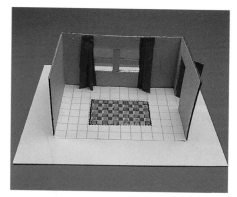

5 Attach the walls along the lines you drew in step 1. Use small pieces of tape on the outside to hold the corners together if needed.

6 When the glue holding the walls together has dried, paint the insides of the walls, the window, and the door to look as real as possible.

7 You may wish to add scraps of fabric for curtains. You could also paint the floor to look like wood or cover it with felt to look like carpet.

Architects and builders often make models of buildings they are going to build. They make the models look as real as possible, with gardens, trees, cars, and even model people. This helps everyone see what the building will look like when it is finished.

NOW TRY THIS

If you enjoyed making this room, you could try making an entire home, with several different rooms. It could be based on the design for a home—see pages 10–11. Or you could make a model of your own home.

ELECTRICITY AT HOME

The amount of electricity that comes into homes is very strong and can be dangerous if not used properly. However, here are ways to learn about electricity, using small batteries and lightbulbs that cannot harm you.

YOU WILL NEED

- Battery (4.5 V minimum)
- Bulbs (3.5 V minimum)
- Bulb holders
- Single-core electrical wire
- Wire strippers and cutters
- Small piece of cardboard
- Scissors
- Paper fasteners

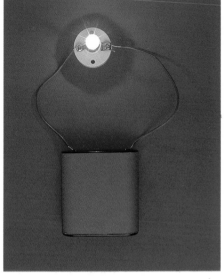

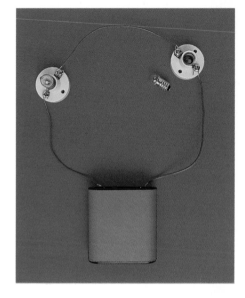

1 Cut two pieces of wire. Strip about 3/4 in. (2 cm) of plastic from each end. Attach one end of each wire to a bulb holder. Place the other ends of the wires on the battery terminals. The bulb should shine brightly.

2 Cut another length of wire so that you can include another bulb in the circuit. Do both bulbs shine? Are they both as bright as the single bulb? Unscrew one bulb. What happens to the other one?

Electricity can be very dangerous if it is not used properly.
- **Never play with electric sockets.**
- **Do not touch or use bare wires.**
- **Never use electricity with wet or damp hands.**

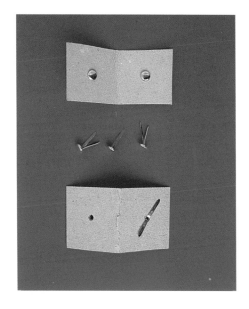 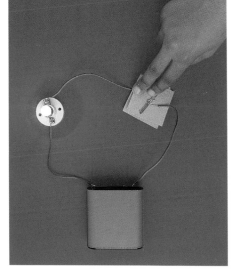 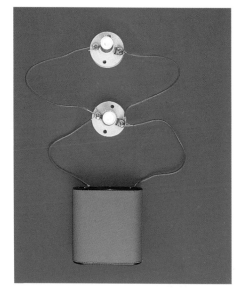

3 Make a switch for the circuit. Cut a small piece of cardboard, about 2 x ³/₄ in. (5 x 2 cm). Make a small hole in each half of the cardboard. Put a paper fastener in each hole with the points on the outside.

4 Twist the bare ends of the wires around the pointed ends of the paper fasteners. Close the switch. The round tops of the paper fasteners should touch, and the bulb should light up. This is called a series circuit.

5 This photo shows a different type of circuit. Put this together with two bulbs. How bright are all the bulbs? Unscrew one bulb. What happens to the others? This is called a parallel circuit.

Electricity gives us power for many different things, such as lights, televisions, stereos, and microwave ovens. People who do not have electricity cannot use these things, and they may have to light their homes at night with oil lamps.

NOW TRY THIS

Lights in homes are made up of parallel circuits. You can put lights in your model room using the small bulbs and a battery.

MODEL FURNITURE

Furniture makes homes more comfortable. We sit on chairs, put things on tables, and keep things in cupboards. Without furniture we would have to sit, eat, and sleep on the ground.

Here is a way to make a model table. Once you have finished it, you can go on to make a whole range of models to go with it.

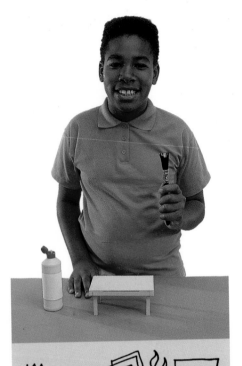

YOU WILL NEED

- 2 ft. (60 cm) wood, approx. 3/4 x 3/4 in. (1 x 1 cm) square
- Thick cardboard
- Glue
- Pencil
- Ruler
- Small hacksaw
- Paint and paintbrush

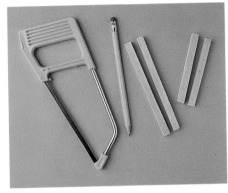

1 Decide on the shape and size of your table. Measure and cut four pieces of wood for the frame of the tabletop.

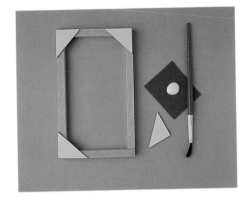

2 Glue the pieces of wood together. It may help to use cardboard triangles so that the corners will be exactly square.

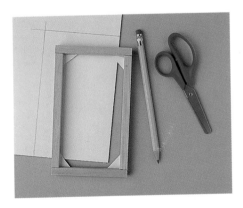

3 When the glue has dried, use the frame to mark out a piece of cardboard for the tabletop. Cut it out and glue it on.

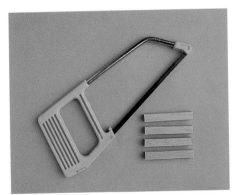

4 Decide how high you want your table to be. Measure this height and cut four equal pieces of wood for the legs.

Dollhouses have been made for hundreds of years. Some were just for children to play with. Others were like works of art with beautiful rooms and dolls. They had furniture that was made exactly like the real thing, only much smaller.

NOW TRY THIS

Now that you know how to cut and join lengths of wood, try making another item of furniture such as a chair to go with the table. Look at real pieces of furniture to see how they are made and try to make them.

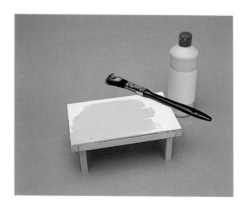

5 Put some glue on the top of each leg and around each inside corner of the frame. Let the glue dry a little and put each leg in place.

6 Paint the table so that it is the same color all over. It could be a bright color, or you could make it look as though it is all made from wood.

17

SOLAR WATER HEATER

Around the world, some homes have hot water, ready to use at any time. It is usually heated by a boiler, using electricity, gas, oil, or coal. But the sun can also make water hot.

YOU WILL NEED

- Lid of a cardboard box
- Clear tubing, about 3/4 in. (8 mm) diameter
- Aluminum foil
- Thin wire (such as single-core electric wire)
- Clear plastic wrap (to cover the lid)
- Tape
- Small plastic funnel
- Plastic modeling clay

1 Take the aluminum foil and line the box lid, covering its bottom and sides. If the foil is loose, fasten it with tape.

2 Measure the box and figure out how much tube you will need for it to go up and down the box a few times.

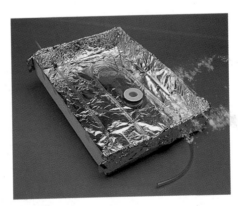

3 Put the tube into the box. Use small pieces of wire that go through the cardboard and tie around the tube. Make holes at either end for the tube to pass out of the box. Cover the box with clear plastic wrap. Attach the plastic wrap at the sides with tape.

4 Put a small ball of modeling clay over the lower end of the tube, to keep the water in. Using a funnel, fill the tube with water. Put another ball of clay over the top end of the tube. Wait for a sunny day and put the box in a window.

5 At the end of the day, take the box out of the window. Take the stopper off the ends of the tube and let the water run out. Test the water to see whether it is warm.

Solar water heaters have panels to catch the heat of the sun. The panels can be put on roofs or on the ground. The sun's energy heats water, which is used for washing and heating. Solar power is used around the world. This system is for a hotel in the Himalayas in Asia.

BUILDING A ROOF

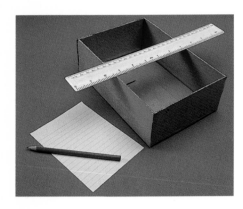

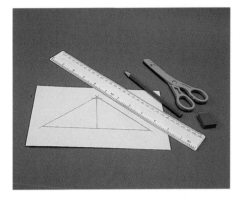

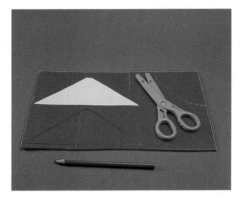

1 Measure across the box. Add on about 3/4 in. (2 cm) to this length so that the roof will hang over the edge on either side. Decide on the height of the roof.

2 Draw a triangle on paper. The bottom will be the length worked out in step 1. Draw a line to cut off the top point. Cut out the paper shape.

3 Use the paper triangle as a template. Mark the shape on the plastic and cut it out. You will need at least four triangles to hold up the roof.

Most buildings have roofs that slope. The angle of the roof helps rain run off to keep it out of the house. A roof that looks like an upside-down V is called a pitched roof.

YOU WILL NEED

- Small cardboard box
- Plastic corrugated sheet (or thick cardboard)
- Cardboard (for roof)
- Glue
- Pencil
- Ruler
- Scissors
- Paint and paintbrush (optional)

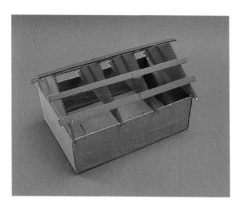

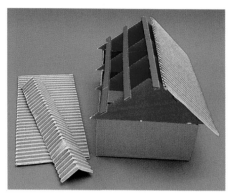

4 Glue the triangles to the top of the box. It will be easiest if you put the glue on, let it dry a little, and then stick the pieces to the box.

5 You need to add rafters to hold the triangles together and support the roof. Measure the length and cut long pieces of plastic. Glue them in place.

6 Add the roof itself. Cut two pieces of cardboard, one for each side. Then cut a V-shaped piece to go over the top. Glue the pieces on, and paint them if you wish.

When a house is being constructed, builders put the walls up first. Then they add the roof. Usually, the roof must have a framework to hold it up. When the frame has been made, the builder covers it with tiles, stone (such as slate), sheets of metal, wood, or even straw.

INUIT IGLOO

The Inuit (also known as Eskimos) live in the freezing, snow-covered parts of Alaska and Canada. Many years ago, they made their homes from blocks of ice—the only material they could find. Here you can make an Inuit dwelling, using sugar cubes instead of ice and cotton instead of snow.

YOU WILL NEED

- Stiff cardboard for base
- Round lid, for drawing a circle
- Pencil
- Box of sugar cubes
- Glue
- Cotton
- Pebbles and gravel (optional)

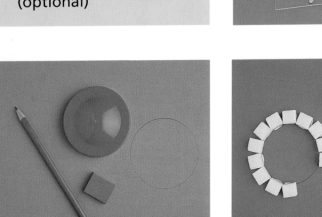

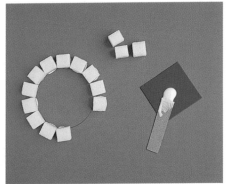

1 Using the round lid and a pencil, draw a circle on the baseboard. This gives you a size and shape to build the igloo.

2 Put a little glue on one side of each cube and place the cubes around the circle. Leave a gap for the door.

3 When a circle is finished, place another on top. To build a dome shape, make each circle smaller than the last.

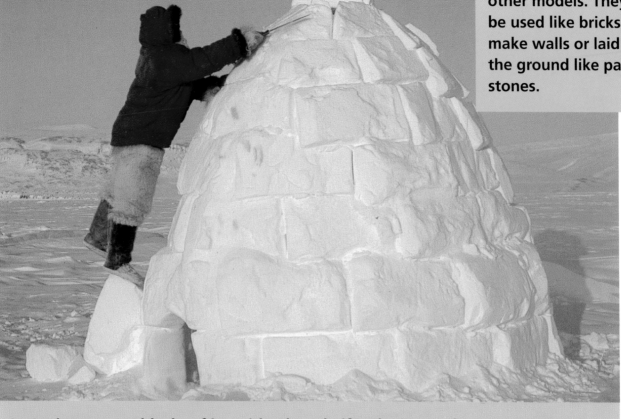

NOW TRY THIS

Use sugar cubes to build other models. They could be used like bricks to make walls or laid flat on the ground like paving stones.

An Inuit man cuts blocks of ice with a long knife. The ice can be cut to make a smooth curved shape. When the blocks are all put together, the builder fills any small holes with smaller pieces of ice or snow. This helps keep the wind out.

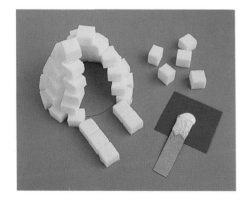

4 When the dome is finished, except for the door space, start to build the tunnel at the front of the igloo.

5 Finish the tunnel. Close the gap above it by gluing on more sugar cubes wherever they are necessary.

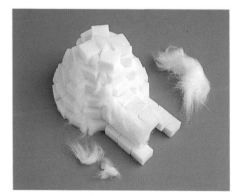

6 Although the igloo shape has now been built, it has many holes between the cubes. Fill these up with cotton.

ARMCHAIR

YOU WILL NEED

- Large amounts of old newspapers
- Old cartons made from thick cardboard
- Strong parcel or packing tape
- Scissors
- Material for covering chair
- Dressmakers' or safety pins

Most chairs are designed for adults to sit in. A grown-up's chair can be uncomfortable for a young person, so here is a way of making a custom-built chair—just for you.

1 Make the seat of the chair from newspapers. Pile up lots of folded papers until you have made a height that is comfortable to sit on. Bind the papers together with parcel tape.

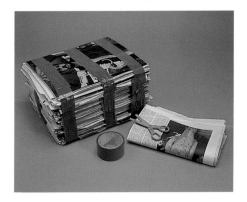

2 Make the back of the chair from thick, stiff cardboard. Cut a piece that is high enough to support your back. Join it to the seat with more tape, making the joins as strong as possible.

Most furniture is made to be as useful as possible. This means that it should be hard to break, easy to clean, and comfortable to use. However, furniture can be interesting to look at—and even fun as well.

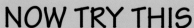

NOW TRY THIS

What did you notice about the rolls of newspaper you made for the arms? When held together tightly with tape, newspapers are very strong. Think of other things you could design and make, using rolled recycled newspapers.

3 Cut lengths of newspaper the same depth as the seat from front to back. Roll them tightly into a tube, and tape them. Attach the tubes to the seat to make arms for the chair.

4 Cover the finished chair with some material. Pin it in place, if necessary, to cover the chair properly.

MINIATURE GARDEN

A beautiful garden should be designed as carefully as the inside of a house. Think of all the things you would like to have in a garden. You might want grass to play on, a tree to climb, or a swing. You could also have a barbecue, a vegetable patch, or a pond.

YOU WILL NEED

- Shallow plastic tray, such as a seed tray
- Sand or gravel
- Flexible garden wire
- Popsicle sticks
- Scraps of cardboard
- Wood glue
- Tissue paper
- Green felt
- 8 x 8 in. (20 x 20 cm) piece of black plastic
- Small pebbles
- Plastic modeling clay

1 Fill the plastic tray with sand or small pieces of gravel, almost to the top. Pack the sand or gravel down and smooth it so that it lies flat.

2 Use wooden twigs, pieces of cardboard, wire, tissue paper, fabric, paint, and modeling clay to make trees, bushes, leaves, and flowers.

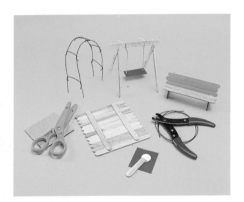

3 Make items such as a fence, bench, swing, wooden "deck," and garden arch from popsicle sticks, cardboard, string, and wire.

4 Use a piece of green felt to look like grass. Cut it to fit and lay it over the gravel. Cut small holes in the felt to "plant" trees and flowers.

Gardens can be used to grow flowers or vegetables or to play in. Some people have very small gardens, just big enough to sit in. Grand houses used to have huge decorative gardens. These needed many people working in them all the time to keep them weeded and trimmed.

6 Arrange all the things you have made in the garden. Make more plants from tissue paper, and paint on flowers. Fill the pond with a little water.

5 You may wish to add a garden pond. Make a hole in the gravel or sand and line it with black plastic. Hold down the plastic with pebbles all around.

A HOME FOR A PET

Animals also have homes. Some live in holes in the ground; others make nests. Animals who are tame and live with us are called pets. Just like us, they need somewhere warm to sleep at night, food, drink, and things to exercise and play with.

YOU WILL NEED

- Plain paper
- Pencil
- Eraser

Imagine you had to design a home for a hamster. Hamsters are small animals. They cannot run around a house like a cat or a dog, because they would get lost or injured. They need safe homes of their own.

Hamsters like somewhere cozy to sleep, such as a box filled with hay or a soft nest.

Hamsters have very strong front teeth. They can gnaw through anything except thick glass, plastic, or metal, so their home must be made from one of these materials. It should be lined with sawdust to make it comfortable.

Pigs on farms are happiest when they can live outdoors. As well as being fed by the farmer, they look for things to eat in the ground. Farmers also make sure they have houses for sleeping and for shelter when the weather is bad.

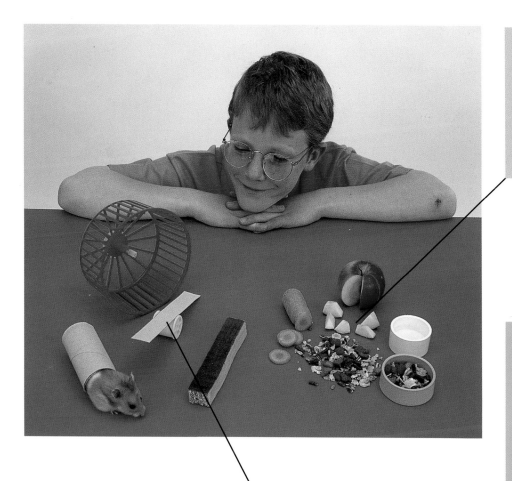

Like all living things, hamsters have to eat and drink. Hamsters like to eat dry seeds, pellets, and fresh food such as apples and carrots.

Now that you know all about how to keep a hamster, draw a picture of an ideal home. It will need separate areas for sleeping, going to the toilet, eating and drinking, and playing. Like people's houses, the hamster's could have two or more floors, with ladders linking them.

Hamsters like things to do and places to explore. Every hamster should have an exercise wheel. Hamsters will also use things like ramps, ladders, branches, jam jars, cardboard tubes, and thread spools.

29

GLOSSARY

architect	A person who designs buildings.
boiler	A machine for heating water.
circuit	An arrangement of things through which an electric current passes.
cube	A shape that has six sides that are all square and the same size.
designing	Getting an idea, planning, and sometimes making a drawing.
dome	A shape that looks like a ball cut in half.
frame	A strong shape that can hold up things put over the top of it.
gnaw	To bite and chew.
hinge	A joint that moves, letting things like doors and windows open and close.
lining	A layer of something inside something else, such as inside a box or hole.
lintel	A piece of wood or stone placed over a door or window to support the wall above.
materials	Things that are used for making and building, such as wood, cement, bricks, glass, fabrics, and so on.
miniature	Something that is much smaller than normal.
model	An object made to look like something that is bigger.
pitched roof	A roof shape that looks like an upside-down V.
rafter	A piece of wood that forms the frame for a roof.
rigid	Describes something that is stiff and hard, which will not bend.
solar	Describes something that uses the sun.
switch	Something that makes and breaks a join in an electric circuit.
template	A shape used to draw around and cut out a number of the same shapes.
tunnel	A long hole, like a tube.
volt (V)	A measurement of the "push," or force, of electricity.
waterproof	Describing something that will not let water pass through it, such as plastic or glass.

BOOKS TO READ

Bare, Colleen S. *This Is a House*. New York: Dutton Children's Press, 1992.

Jackson, Mike. *Homes Around the World*. Read All About It. Austin, TX: Raintree Steck-Vaughn, 1995.

Lambert, Mark. *Homes in the Future*. Houses and Homes. Minneapolis, MN: Lerner Group, 1989.

Oxlade, Chris. *Houses and Homes*. Technology Craft Topics. Danbury, CT: Franklin Watts, 1994.

Walker, Lester. *Housebuilding for Children*. New York: Overlook Press, 1990.

Wilkinson, Phillip. *Building*. Eyewitness. New York: Alfred A. Knopf, 1995.

ADDITIONAL NOTES

Native American Teepee, "Mud" House, and Inuit Igloo These three houses are examples of how to make the best use of the materials available. A traditional teepee, although easily carried about, was very strong when erected. The mud and ice used for the two other houses represent the extremes of the climate that exist in these areas. Children may build these projects to give them the opportunity to develop their technological skills, experiment with a range of structures, and provide cross-curricular topics for linking into geography and other cultures.

Design a Home It is often difficult for children to design structures or models without first having experience of the materials with which they would need to build. They should be allowed as much freedom as possible to make imaginative designs, but at the same time be encouraged to be precise and accurate, and where possible, work to a scale.

Model Room Children should be encouraged to keep their designs simple because they will form the base for their models. Because the cardboard should be as rigid as possible, young children may need help with the cutting and gluing. Making scale models is often part of the process from the drawing board to the finished product.

Electricity at Home Children need to be made aware of the dangers of electricity, and this project could also give them the opportunity to design suitable posters about this, as well as the importance of saving energy in the home and at school.

Model Furniture Although this design is being used to make a model table, this basic structure can also be a part of many other projects. The combination of square section wood and cardboard corners will also form a very rigid structure to make buildings, towers, and bridges.

Building a Roof Supports for a pitched roof would normally be a hollow structure. One of the problems with a triangular structure of this kind is that over the years the weight of the roof will gradually widen the base of the triangle. Children should be encouraged to understand these "real life" problems.

Solar Water Heater When investigating the water system, children should be made aware that solar heating is an important secondary source of energy that requires no destruction of primary resources such as coal, gas, or oil.

Armchair This project will enable children to carry out a simple ergonomic study. This looks at how people relate to their working environment and how conditions can be adapted to fit the individual to obtain the maximum efficiency. Children should be encouraged to think about how a chair should not only look good, but also support the body with a minimum of stress and a maximum of comfort.

Miniature Garden, Home for a Pet These projects help to develop the concept of a home beyond the confines of four walls and a roof. The projects give plenty of scope for designing and using a variety of materials imaginatively.

INDEX

Acknowledgments

The author and publishers wish to thank the following for their kind assistance with this book:
models Abdullah Crawford, Josie Kearns, Hugh Williams, Juliet Williams, Yasmin Mukhida and Rebecca Thomas. Also A. Coombes (Pet Supplies, Brighton), Sylph Baier, Cathy Baxter, and Gus Ferguson.

For the use of their library photographs, grateful thanks are due to:
Bryan and Cherry Alexander p. 23; Chapel Studios p. 17 (Graham Horner), p. 27 (Tim Richardson); Eye Ubiquitous p. 10 (K. Wilton), p. 29 (Paul Seheult); Photri Inc p. 5 (Tracy Wetherby), p. 6 (John Robert McCauley), p. 13 (Richard Nowitz), p. 21; Topham Picturepoint pp. 5 and 25. All other photographs belong to the Wayland Picture Library.